MW01233098

YOU
Deserve
IT

A 30-Day Curriculum Guide to Social and Emotional Learning

MYCHAL A. WINTERS, ED.S.

YOU DESERVE IT
A 30-Day Curriculum Guide to Social and Emotional Learning

ISBN (978-0-578-85368-0)

Preface

Teaching during a pandemic has changed the dynamics of teaching and learning. In-person learning allows all scholars to have access to a stable learning environment where they will receive high-quality instruction from highly qualified teachers. They also receive daily affirmations and social and emotional support. Some families can continue to provide that same structure and support at home. Then there are some that lack structure and support and their children struggle. Virtual learning brought about significant changes for educators, scholars, and their families.

This curriculum was designed with scholars, families, and those seeking to better themselves in mind. It is an ideal resource to supplement curriculums in schools, mentoring programs, learning centers, churches, etc. This curriculum can be read one prompt at a time, one section at a time, or self-paced. The prompts are very direct and meant to provoke deeper thought and conversation around the topic. This curriculum is a guide to social and emotional development because it asks probing questions that require the reader to examine their social and emotional state of being and make action steps toward development.

Introduction

You Deserve It: Curriculum Guide for Social and Emotional Learning explores five principles that bring awareness of social and emotional needs that enable every learner to realize the existence of their highest potential. The model displays the relationship between the fundamental needs of stability, self-love, resilience, discovery, and purpose.

In this curriculum, stability is the foundation for the realization of one's highest potential. The desire to be protected, cared for, properly educated, heard, healthy, and to have structure adds to stability. Stability in those areas are key to developing socially and emotionally. When stability is not accessible, it is recommended to get support from a reliable source. That can be a close friend or relative, counselor, school, place of worship, shelter, school, etc.

Self-love is a foundational principle because it enables each individual to value themselves and be able to value others. Self-care is a form of self-love which is critical to establishing balanced emotional health.

Resilience is a fundamental principle that requires stability and self-love. To recover from traumatic experiences, one must have a self-realization that they deserve more and that they deserve the opportunity to progress beyond the traumatic experiences they have endured. Stability is needed to provide the context and means to be resilient.

Discovery is the second-highest level of realizing one's highest potential. Discovery involves the process of discovering new interests, becoming aware of the world, and self-reflection.

The highest level of potential is purpose. When each core principle is aligned, it leads to purpose. Purpose is also vicariously embedded in the other principles. When one is aware that they have a purpose and reach the understanding that where they currently are in life and their social and emotional state is part of their purpose, they can operate in their highest potential. In this curriculum, purpose is an interactive principle, meaning that purposes shift according to life's positioning.

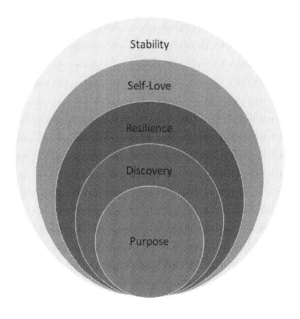

Table of Contents

Principle I: Stability

You Deserve to be Protected
You Deserve to be Cared For
You Deserve to be Healthy
You Deserve Structure
You Deserve to be Educated Properly
You Deserve to be Heard

You Deserve to Be Protected

Being protected is one of the most secure feelings that provides a sense of stability. The most successful and productive people know to protect what is valuable to them. The wealthy protect their investments, parents protect their children, athletes wear certain types of equipment to protect their bodies. In the game of chess, the King is the piece protected the most because it is the key to victory. Most types of electronic devices come with protection, whether it be for the device itself or for the software. When our most valuable assets are protected, we experience the highest level of stability. It provides a sense of security that enables us to operate with confidence, knowing we are safe.

As it relates to social and emotional development, it is important to protect your interests, thoughts, and feelings. People experience life in dynamically different ways, which lead to diverse experiences and outcomes. Depending on your demographic, you may live in a geographical area or neighborhood that is more or less protected than others. This could result in exposure to traumatic experiences. As much as we would like to protect ourselves and our loved ones from all hurt, harm, and danger some things we cannot escape. Ultimately, we are not in control of many external factors. We are, however, in control of every intrinsic factor.

Regardless of your life experiences, you are deserving of protection and stability in every aspect of your life. Be vigilant of your thoughts. Your thoughts are powerful and shape your reality, regardless of what is going on in the world around you. Learn to protect what is important to you. Develop strategies on how to protect your mental and emotional health (healthy, research-based strategies).

- What is valuable to you?
- What areas in your life do you feel lack of stability due to lack of protection?
- How can you protect your thoughts and feelings?
- What areas of your life do you frequently think about guarding?
- Why are those areas highly guarded?

- How do your actions affect others around you?

YOU DESERVE IT

You Deserve to Be Cared For

I can recall being sick as a young child and my Granny would check on me frequently, making sure that I had everything that I needed to feel better. She made sure that I had plenty of fluids and soups and was taking my prescribed medication. One time, she had the church choir come over to sing to me to lift my spirits. That was very special and very kind of them to take the time out to do that. As a child, I did not know how to respond to that act of kindness. I wasn't used to that and had never seen it done before; I actually felt overstimulated in the moment and didn't know what to do, so I turned around while they were singing. That wasn't the proper way to respond, and thankfully no one took offense to my gesture because they knew that I was not feeling well and that I was a child that didn't know better. Looking back, I realize how I pushed away acts of kindness and care because I did not know how to respond.

Growing up, I was very self-sufficient. I thought I knew how to take care of myself and did not need anyone to help me. That attitude caused me to push people away and I struggled to accept care from others. The word is called pride, and it is highly destructive. Do not allow pride to push people that care about you away. Instead, allow people to care for you in the way they authentically choose to. We cannot control how people express their care and concern for us, but we can identify their efforts and accept them. You deserve to accept care and concern from people who genuinely want to see you well. It may seem uncomfortable to you and you may not know how to respond. The best way to respond is thankfulness, because they did not have to care at all. When you can allow others to care for you, you can develop a sense of stability. You can identify who is truly in your corner for support.

- How do you respond when people go out of their way to care for you?
- Do you have a hard time accepting care from others?
- What are the blocks that prevent you from receiving care from others?
- In what ways do you prefer to receive care from others?

- How can you acknowledge the efforts of others that show concern and care for your wellbeing?

YOU DESERVE IT

_____

_____

_____

_____

_____

_____

_____

_____

_____

_____

_____

You Deserve to Be Healthy

Having a healthy body, thoughts, and relationships contribute to having a sense of stability. When we are healthy, we can operate on our highest level. Is it possible to have stability when we are not healthy? My answer is yes. My answer is yes because there must be a balance when you are not healthy. Though we may experience various types of illnesses or injuries, our hearts and minds can carry us through. An individual with a positive mindset and determined spirit can find balance regardless of their physical state. It can be a challenge to stay positive and in good spirits when dealing with serious illnesses and injuries, but it is the key to healing and living a balanced life. I am reminded of a verse from Proverbs that says, "A healthy spirit conquers adversity, but what can you do when the spirit is crushed?" Your mindset is key to overcoming any physical, mental, or relational challenge. Protect your peace, guard your thoughts, and practice healthy habits daily to recover.

- What areas of your life require healing?

- What are your thoughts about those areas?
- What habits can you practice daily to improve/maintain your health in those areas?

_____

_____

_____

_____

_____

_____

_____

_____

_____

_____

_____

_____

You Deserve to Be Educated Properly

It is one thing to be educated, but another thing to be educated properly. In an era where we have unlimited access to information and opinions on social media are presented as facts, it is critical to establish a true understanding. The spread of misinformation and bias has led to unnecessary conflict. As a college student, I learned the importance of validating the source of information. Any information referenced in an essay must come from a reputable source. I see false information being shared on social media daily ,and unfortunately, the people who share the information rarely check the source before sharing the information with others. I read countless posts from others that lead to them sharing their thoughts and reactions from that information. When receiving information, always question the source and the person providing the information to make sure that you are not receiving biased or inaccurate information. A proper education leads to wise decisions being made. If the information you receive does not help you make wise or better decisions or more informed decisions, continue to research the information.

As it relates to educational institutions, you cannot solely rely on school systems or programs to teach you everything you need to know. Unfortunately, those systems are flawed and inequitable often. Take advantage of the resources around you to help bridge gaps.

- What are some resources that you have available to you that will help you become more educated on a topic of interest?
- How often do you check the source of information you share on the internet?
- How often have you allowed misinformation to impact your mood or feelings?

Mychal A. Winters, Ed.S

_____

_____

_____

_____

_____

_____

_____

_____

_____

_____

_____

_____

You Deserve to Be Heard

There is comfort in knowing that your voice matters. That sense of comfort brings peace and stability in being heard. I am reminded of the most recent wave of activism, the Black Lives Matter movement, is more than a hashtag. Over the past few years, many have used their social media platforms to shine a light on racial inequities as it relates to police brutality and unjust treatment of blacks and minorities. The movement is more than a hashtag and social media post. It is the voice of the people who are tired of seeing history repeat itself. It is the voice of the people who are fed up with seeing countless unarmed black men and women being killed by law enforcement. It is the voice of those who are seeking the comfort of true justice. Black lives matter does not mean that other lives don't matter. It means that these are the lives that are being unjustly taken at a disproportionately higher rate than others. Those voices deserve to be heard. Your voice deserves to be heard. Do not be silent on the issues that matter to you.

- What are some social issues that you or those around you are vocal about?
- What do you notice about those who are silent about the issues important to you?
- How can your voice be heard?

_____

_____

_____

_____

_____

_____

_____

_____

_____

_____

_____

_____

Principle II: Self-Love

You Deserve to Love
You Deserve to be Loved
You Deserve to Find Yourself
You Deserve Self-Care
You Deserve Commitment
You Deserve Healing

You Deserve to Love

A part of self-love is giving the love you desire. I believe in the law of attraction and that the energy we put out is the energy we will attract. If you desire to attract a certain type of love or reaction, be sure that you exemplify it. Giving the love and energy you desire is a way to reward yourself because it will come back to you. I look at acts of love and kindness as investments. There is a misconception you cannot give something that you've never had. I believe that we must become the change we want to see. We must embody and exemplify love every chance we get.

- Are you receiving the love you desire?
- How do you show love to others?
- How do you show love to yourself?
- What are some small "investments" that you can make to impact those around you?

YOU DESERVE IT

_____

_____

_____

_____

_____

_____

_____

_____

_____

_____

_____

_____

You Deserved to Be Loved

One of the most fundamental human needs is the need to be loved and feel loved. The desire to be loved comes with unique needs. Each person receives and gives love in different ways. Naturally, we seek love from our family, friends, and romantic interests. Some spend the majority of their lives searching for the love they felt they did not receive from friends, family, and romantic interests. I believe that it is possible to feel loved even more by accepting love how it is given. We often want to receive love the way that we want it, but it rarely comes packaged the way we prefer it. It's challenging to find someone able to give love in a way in which you desire to receive it. If you are fortunate enough to find someone willing to learn how to give you the love you desire and deserve, that is a person you should keep close.

- What is your love language?
- What are ways you desire to be loved?
- Who are the people in your life you seek love from?

- Who are the people in your life that consistently show or try to give you the love you desire?

_____

_____

_____

_____

_____

_____

_____

_____

_____

_____

_____

_____

You Deserve to Find Yourself

During the lifelong process of learning ourselves, you deserve to find yourself in each stage of life. As the demands of life change and require a different version of yourself, your interests and needs will change. Finding yourself simply means to fully explore and develop your interests. Sometimes finding yourself means letting go of things that no longer serve you well. It is not uncommon to outgrow certain habits, desires, and patterns. It is very healthy to outgrow habits that no longer serve you. When you mindlessly engage in certain behaviors and activities, it is time to reflect on the purpose of it in your life.

- What are some new interests that you have discovered in this season of your life?
- What are some habits that no longer serve you well that you can let go?

YOU DESERVE IT

_____

_____

_____

_____

_____

_____

_____

_____

_____

_____

_____

You Deserve Self-Care

One of the most refreshing feelings is walking out of the barbershop with a fresh haircut. It truly does elevate my spirit. You deserve to do something daily that is a form of self-care. Some people enjoy going to the spa, salon, barbershop, trying a new restaurant, recipe, shopping, reading, exercising, drawing, painting, and other activities as a form of self-care. Take some "me-time" as a form of self-care. Self-care is a form of self-love because you are intentionally making time to cater to your own needs in your own unique way. It is easy to get caught up in meeting the demands of work, school, and others and lose balance. Self-care is a way to restore and maintain balance.

- Do you regularly practice self-care?
- What are some ways that you practice self-care?
- Are there any areas in your life that are out of balance?
- How can you restore balance in those areas?

YOU DESERVE IT

_____

_____

_____

_____

_____

_____

_____

_____

_____

_____

_____

You Deserve Commitment

Commitment is a form of self-love because it involves being connected to something larger than yourself. Commitment works two ways: giving and receiving. You must commit yourself to things that will help you grow and develop mentally, emotionally, socially, spiritually, financially, and physically. To understand the principle of commitment, you must fully engage in it. When you are aware of what it takes to be committed to something, you will appreciate the commitment you receive from others. You can also identify those who aren't as committed as you are to something, and determine which steps are necessary going forward.

- What are some things that you are committed to?
- What areas could you be more committed to?
- Does your level of commitment align with your expectations of others?

_____

_____

_____

_____

_____

_____

_____

_____

_____

_____

_____

_____

You Deserve Healing

Sometimes we endure unexpected injuries, setbacks, breakups, and disappointments. Some of those unexpected experiences can be detrimental and devastating. Unfortunately, everyone has not been able to heal and recover. You deserve healing in all the areas you have experienced pain and brokenness. Without healing, it will be a struggle to operate at your highest capacity and perform to the best of your abilities. That can apply to physical and emotional healing. As a former athlete, I have witnessed how injured athletes have tried to come back to the game while they were still hurt and their performance suffered because of it. Sometimes, their injuries were worse because of it. Not taking the time to heal could also damage your future. It is a form of self-love to allow yourself the proper time to heal and work through any physical or emotional damage so you can return better and perform better. Depending on the type of hurt or injury, the healing process can take longer and healing will have different phases. You deserve to go through the process and become a better you.

- What are some things that you are healing from?
- How can you be intentional about embracing the healing process?
- What patterns do you find yourself in when you try to engage in certain activities too soon?

_____

_____

_____

_____

_____

_____

_____

_____

_____

_____

_____

_____

Principle III: Resilience

You Deserve to Make Mistakes
You Deserve to Learn from Mistakes
You Deserve to Learn from Disappointment
You Deserve Accountability
You Deserve to Grow
You Deserve Another Chance

You Deserve to Make Mistakes

As an educator, I witness scholars work so hard each year to make good grades. Every year they deal with the pressure of performing the best with a low margin for error. I strongly dislike that the educational system categorizes learners based on their performance on an assessment that does not measure the essence of their true potential and ability. This performance-based mindset contributes to people being afraid to make mistakes. People often equate mistakes with failure. This cannot be further from the truth. Mistakes provide a pathway to success. Most mistakes can be corrected while others can be more costly. But you deserve to live and learn through those mistakes. No one knows everything about anything and no one is perfect.

- What are you hesitant about doing because you are afraid to make a mistake?

YOU DESERVE IT

_____

_____

_____

_____

_____

_____

_____

_____

_____

_____

_____

You Deserve to Learn from Mistakes

Failure results from not learning from mistakes and not trying. My grandfather used to always tell me, "Nothing beats a failure but a try." That means that the only way you can fail is if you do not try. Many people are discouraged from trying new things and pursuing their goals because they are afraid to make mistakes and fail. Making mistakes is a part of life. Do not be held back in fear of making a mistake. Take the first step and learn the lessons along the way. If you make a mistake, it is critical to learn from it. Identify what went wrong and what the factors were that contributed to it. When you do not learn from mistakes, you must continue to revisit the situation until you learn the lesson. Instead of feeling down and being hard on yourself for messing up, write down the details about the issue and write down the actions or lack of actions you were responsible for. Make a plan on how you will approach the situation differently when you revisit it. In the words of my grandfather, "you will see this again."

- What are some mistakes that you have learned from?
- What are some mistakes that you have made that you are still trying to overcome?
- How can you make corrections to your actions and mindset so you will not have to repeat the same mistakes?

_____

_____

_____

_____

_____

_____

_____

_____

_____

_____

_____

_____

You Deserve to Learn from Disappointment

One thing we cannot escape in life is disappointment. Because people are imperfect, people will often disappoint us. Because we cannot control external circumstances, there will be things that will not always go our way, which will lead to other disappointments. One way to be proactive and reduce the effects of disappointment is to remove expectations. Placing expectations on people and situations is the quickest way to set yourself up for disappointment. Expectations put us in a position to require a level of performance or ntee. It puts the external party in control. When dealing with disappointment, be intentional about accepting the outcome and freeing yourself of expectations

YOU DESERVE IT

_____

_____

_____

_____

_____

_____

_____

_____

_____

_____

_____

_____

You Deserve Accountability

Being resilient means being able to recover and make a comeback after a difficult or undesirable situation. Being held accountable for your actions and thoughts enables you to recover more efficiently. It is human nature to rely on our own way of doing things. When our way has proved to be ineffective, we need systems in place to help us be more accountable for our shortcomings. When you are serious about getting results, you will look for effective systems and methods to help you progress. Life has a way of putting people in our path working toward the same goals. They can be your accountability partner without you even revealing it. Pay attention to the habits of those who succeed at what you are working toward. Don't be afraid to ask questions and ask for help. No one started off at the top. Be willing to learn from others.

- In what areas are you undisciplined and need accountability?

YOU DESERVE IT

_____

_____

_____

_____

_____

_____

_____

_____

_____

_____

_____

You Deserve to Grow

I think that it is fascinating that everything that has been created by The Creator was only made once and then perpetually reproduced. Each living thing has its own life cycle. Within those cycles are patterns of growth. As humans, we are perpetually growing and moving physically. Physical growth is inevitable but can be limited based on the dietary intake. Spiritual, mental, and emotional growth is not so inevitable. Those areas require focused and intentional habits for growth to occur. This is why some younger people are more intelligent and mature than grown adults. Their internal development has not caught up with their external development. Growth is attainable when you learn to shift your low vibrational thoughts to higher thoughts. A shift in mindset can very well lead to a shift in your reality. You deserve to grow. Be intentional on what you are feeding yourself the right things for growth to take place.

- What areas of your life would you like to grow?

- How can you shift your mindset to see the growth and possibility in each situation?
- What are some experiences that have required you to change your thinking?

You Deserve Another Chance

Part of being resilient is overcoming adversity. When you overcome a difficult situation, you position yourself to have a new start with a new perspective. Whatever it is that you have endured, you came out of it and now you have a new level of insight and strength. Do not allow that difficult experience to go to waste! Apply what you have learned in your new season. A new start with a new perspective is the key to success. It is very rare that people reach the highest level of success from their first attempt or after their first failure. Fall in love with the process and never tire of starting over. Do not allow the criticism of those who have not tried to pursue their goals to hinder you from starting over. Take as many chances as you need to get it right.

- What is a goal you have recently failed to reach? Is it worth starting over?
- If it is worth starting the process over, what steps will you take to reach a different outcome?

YOU DESERVE IT

_____

_____

_____

_____

_____

_____

_____

_____

_____

_____

_____

Principle IV: Discovery

You Deserve to be Active
You Deserve to Participate
You Deserve to Explore
You Deserve to Achieve
You Deserve to See the World
You Deserve to Be Part of Something Bigger
than Yourself

You Deserve to be Active

One way to discover your interests is to get active. Find new activities and organizations to be a part of. Being active creates networking opportunities, which can open the door to lifelong connections. In college, I was a member of an academic organization that one professor encouraged me to join. I was hesitant about joining because none of the members looked like me. After I joined, I met people who came from different backgrounds but were working towards the same goals. The door was open for me to network and make connections that my other peers didn't have access to. Through the organization, I could travel to places I had never been before and attend workshops that gave me resources that would be helpful for years to come. I met students and professors from all across the country I have developed strong relationships with. I still have professors from other colleges contact me to see how I am and to let me know about career opportunities. If I simply stayed in my dorm room playing video games, I would have missed out on these amazing opportunities.

- How can you be more active at your school, job, organization, etc.?
- How can you build meaningful relationships with others from different backgrounds?

_____

_____

_____

_____

_____

_____

_____

_____

_____

_____

_____

_____

You Deserve to Participate

I can remember attending school dances and other social events and just staying to myself and standing on the wall in the back. I would watch everyone else have the time of their lives while I was too afraid to go and enjoy myself. My excuse was that I was shy and reserved. The truth was that I was afraid of people's opinion of me enjoying myself. In the past, I allowed the fear of people's opinions to stop me from doing many things I was genuinely interested in. Do not allow the fear of what others think stop you from being great. I have learned that what other people think of me is none of my business. Don't allow your life to be on hold due to fear of being judged.

- How has the fear or concern of people's opinion affected your decisions?
- Why do you value people's opinion of you?

YOU DESERVE IT

_____

_____

_____

_____

_____

_____

_____

_____

_____

_____

_____

You Deserve to Explore

My family and I used to travel frequently when I was in grade school. My parents used to take my sister and I, and occasionally other family members, on a summer vacation every summer. My interests developed the more that we traveled. When I was younger, I was more interested in the theme parks and games. As I got older and more accustomed to certain things, I became more interested in music, sports, and fashion. As I continued to mature, I asked about intellectual things such as books, colleges, and artwork. I am thankful to have parents able to expose me to the world and provide opportunities to stimulate my interests. The best way to explore your interests is to start where you are. Before we were able to take a trip every summer, we would visit the local parks and monuments, libraries, festivals, churches, restaurants, and sports events. I had to explore my interests locally before I could appreciate the resources in other places. Now, we can explore our interests with a simple Google search. Nothing beats going new places and trying new things, but we have the resources to learn and explore new things without spending any money. Use your resources wisely.

- What are some interests that you would like to explore if money was not a factor?
- How can you explore your interests locally?

You Deserve to Achieve

One of my favorite experiences as an educator is seeing how proud scholars and their families are to attend awards programs. When scholars learn that they will be receiving an award for their academic achievements, their countenance lights up and there's usually a burst of excitement. On award day, they come to school dressed up with a look of distinction and their families come to support them and take dozens of pictures. Some parents take the time out to share how much their scholar had to overcome outside of school and how they had many challenges that could have prevented them from doing well. Some of the stories leave me in awe because, based on the work they do and the way they carry themselves, I had no clue what they were dealing with at home. That makes the achievement even more special. It also allows me to appreciate their celebrations even more. Achievement leads to celebration. The celebration of achievement motivates some to continue to achieve. Life can be challenging for everyone. It is those who persevere through the struggle and continue to perform with excellence that value achievement the most.

- What are some achievements that you have recently been acknowledged for?
- In what areas can you apply more focus and effort to achieve your goals?

_____

_____

_____

_____

_____

_____

_____

_____

_____

_____

_____

_____

You Deserve to See the World

Most people have a list of places where they would like to visit. If you can travel and see different parts of the world, you are very fortunate. During my travels, I have learned to shift my perspective from a traveler to consider what life is like for the locals of the area. This has helped shape my perspective of the world. It has helped me understand what different cultures value along with the common values we share. With this view, I can categorize what is essential and what is not. The people around you are very influential in what you determine to be important. If you lived in another part of the country or another part of the world, would it still be as important?

- Where are some places that you would like to travel if you had the chance?
- If you have traveled, what are some similarities and differences in the values of the people there?

YOU DESERVE IT

_____

_____

_____

_____

_____

_____

_____

_____

_____

_____

_____

_____

You Deserve to Be Part of Something Bigger Than Yourself

One of the most fundamental needs is the sense of belonging. We were created to contribute to a greater cause than ourselves. Some people are naturally outgoing and enjoy being around people. Others can be more to themselves and not like people as much. Regardless of your disposition, there is someone else in the world who needs what you have. Your presence is a blessing to someone on this earth. Your ideas, experiences, and creativity are needed to help contribute to a greater common good. Those who need it will never benefit if you are closed-off and feel like your presence doesn't matter. It may be uncomfortable, but push yourself to be connected to a person, group, or organization that could use what you have. The connections are priceless.

- What opportunities do you have to share your gifts with others?
- How can you be impactful in the life of at least one person?

YOU DESERVE IT

_____

_____

_____

_____

_____

_____

_____

_____

_____

_____

Principle V: Purpose

You Deserve to Dream
You Deserve to Have a Plan
You Deserve to Grind
You Deserve to Be Effective
You Deserve Hope
You Deserve Opportunities

Mychal A. Winters, Ed.S

You Deserve to Dream

One of the most powerful abilities we have as humans is the ability to dream. Dreams are bridges between our desires and reality. I have the highest level of respect for those who have turned their dreams into reality because, as a dreamer, I know how difficult it can be to work towards them. Having a dream is free, but pursuing it will cost you. Depending on how big the dream is and how intentional you are about working on it, it can be more costly. I am an advocate for dreaming responsibly. That means you should analyze if your dream glorifies self or will help humanity. When you work on pursuing a dream, your focus and energy must align with the direction of that dream. While you work on your dreams, many obstacles could try to discourage you. If you are aware of the power of your dream, nothing will deter you.

- What is something that you have always dreamt of doing?
- What have been some obstacles you had to overcome while pursuing a dream?

YOU DESERVE IT

_____

_____

_____

_____

_____

_____

_____

_____

_____

_____

_____

You Deserve to Have a Plan

Preparation is key to walking in your purpose. Always have a plan ready. Even if things do not go as planned, prepare as if it would. When you get an opportunity to do something that you have always dreamt of, make sure that you are ready to operate in that capacity. My philosophy is that an opportunity is only an opportunity when you are ready for it. Dream big and plan accordingly. Be ready when your name is called.

- How are you preparing for the things you dream and pray about?
- How can you make your plans more strategic?

YOU DESERVE IT

_____

_____

_____

_____

_____

_____

_____

_____

_____

_____

_____

_____

You Deserve to Grind

Dreams do not work unless you do! Some people use faith as an excuse for poor work ethic and lack of research. Whatever you intend to do with your life, work hard until you see it through! No one will do the work for you. The grind not only helps you get closer to where you want to be, but it also brings respect. It makes you appreciate the things you are working toward and it also makes those around you respect you and your craft. People can tell who truly put the work in and those who do just enough. Allow your work to speak for itself.

- What areas can you put forth more effort?
- How can you improve the quality of your work?

YOU DESERVE IT

_____

_____

_____

_____

_____

_____

_____

_____

_____

_____

_____

_____

You Deserve to Be Effective

When we walk in purpose, it is to be able to serve others. To truly serve others, we must be effective at what we do. Being effective requires you to do what is needed instead of doing what you feel is needed or what you want to do. To be an effective educator, I must teach to meet the needs of the scholars based on their individual needs. It would not be effective for me to come to class and just share random information because I can. Being effective also means being adaptable. If what you are doing is not working, you must change it up.

- What is something that you do that is highly effective?
- How can you be more attentive to the needs of those that you serve to be more effective?

YOU DESERVE IT

_____

_____

_____

_____

_____

_____

_____

_____

_____

_____

You Deserve Hope

One of my favorite Proverbs says, "hope deferred makes the heart sick." When we don't get to see the things we hope for, it can be very discouraging. Sometimes all that it takes to keep us motivated is to see evidence of what we are hoping for. Hope is the belief in the goodwill that the things we desire will manifest. Do not give up hope on what you have been believing in. Sometimes it takes longer to see the evidence. During the waiting time, allow your faith to grow.

- What are some things that you are hopeful for?

YOU DESERVE IT

_____

_____

_____

_____

_____

_____

_____

_____

_____

_____

_____

You Deserve Opportunity

Some of the most talented people were not aware of how talented they were until they received an opportunity to showcase their skills. When given the opportunity to do something, it will reveal how talented you are and how dedicated you are. It is easy to say what we would do if given the opportunity, but when the opportunity presents itself, people get a true reflection of their capabilities.

Sometimes opportunity comes disguised as something that we never had a desire to do. Expand your horizons and don't be afraid to try new things. You never know what they could lead to. It's stressful to feel as if you are not prepared for a certain opportunity. A positive thought that can reaffirm your worth is that opportunities are given to those that deserve them. Do not allow the pressure to cause you to disqualify yourself.

- What are some current opportunities you are seeking?
- How have you handled unique opportunities in the past?

YOU DESERVE IT

_____

_____

_____

_____

_____

_____

_____

_____

_____

_____

_____

_____

Reflection

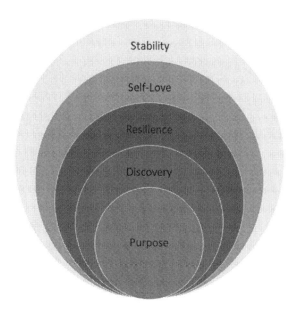

1. Which principle is the most relatable for you in this season of your life?
2. Which principle would you like to dedicate more attention to? What are three action steps you can take to do it?
3. How do you exhibit these five principles to others?
4. Which area have you observed the most personal growth in the past month, 6 months, and year?

About the Author

Author Mychal A. Winters, Ed.S. is an educator in Memphis, TN. Winters began his journey as an educator in 2011 as a paraprofessional in his hometown of Vicksburg, MS. It was there where he discovered his passion for working with students. He earned a Bachelor of Science in Elementary Education (2015) and Master of Education in Elementary Education (2017) from Delta State University. In 2019, he earned a Specialist in Educational Administration and Leadership from The University of Southern Mississippi. In 2019, Winters founded Winters Literacy LLC, which is an educational business that provides services such as tutoring, mentoring, books and curriculum, and podcasts.

Connect

www.wintersliteracy.org

info@wintersliteracy.org

Follow

Instagram: @thegrowtheducator

YouTube: The Growth Educator

Wins & Lessons Podcast

Made in the USA
Middletown, DE
19 June 2021

42192366R00055